MW01504851

Sailing
America

TO MY KIDS—READ, BILLY, AND ADRIAN

Sailing America

ONNE VAN DER WAL | INTRODUCTION BY GARY JOBSON

RIZZOLI
NEW YORK

CONTENTS

INTRODUCTION

The remarkable thing about being on or near the water is how swiftly the weather, the light, and the environment change. You can't see the wind, but you can see the effect the wind has on boats and the water. Onne van der Wal, one of the world's best and most productive marine photographers, has studied and photographed the ever-changing sea for nearly forty years. He raced as a crew member aboard the winning yacht *Flyer* in the 1981–82 Whitbread Round the World Race.

Onne was at sea in that 1981–82 race for 119 days on four different legs, and the *Flyer* set a new record for racing around the world. Aboard the *Flyer*, twenty-five-year-old Onne was on the normal routine of standing a watch of four hours on and four hours off. That gave him the opportunity to observe a wide variety of weather conditions ranging from fierce storms in the Southern Ocean (also known as the Antarctic Ocean) to no wind at all in the doldrums near the equator. Through this maze of weather and water, Onne watched as his fellow crewmates continuously shifted gears to deal with every change in the weather. As one might imagine, it must have been quite an emotional roller-coaster ride for the crew of *Flyer* to push their yacht to the limit and eventually to win the race in the process. During the Whitbread, Onne van der Wal was inspired to make a career out of photographing the sea, the sky, yachts, points of land, and the sailors who have such a strong passion for being on the water. We are lucky that he has given us a many-decades-long visual treasury of extraordinary images to enjoy.

The Whitbread Round the World Race was a career-defining moment for Onne van der Wal. His onboard duties included serving as the bowman and as the yacht's engineer. In addition to those arduous tasks, he also took many pictures throughout the race, capturing astounding images that told the story of what it was like to race around the globe. Most sailors dream about sailing across oceans; through Onne's compelling visual narratives, we learn what such adventures are actually all about. Since completing the Whitbread, he has taken well over one million pictures. His work has appeared in countless magazines and proudly hangs on the walls of many homes and offices. These photographs do not happen by accident. Onne has the unique ability to anticipate the special angle that captures his subject matter with a perspective that might only exist for a split second.

Sailing America is the latest in a series of books featuring Onne van der Wal's work. The chapters are organized by regions established by the United States Sailing Association, the governing body of sailing in the United States. In these chapters, we encounter many different types of boats, and the shoreline terrain, the color of the water, the shape of waves, and even the expressions on sailors' faces create an eclectic look at sailing in America. Great images should make a singular statement when you first look at them. Onne's images provide an easy, yet stunning style. Spend some time examining these photographs, and you will discover fascinating details. Every boat seems to invite the viewer on board. You can sense the motion of the yacht through the water. The symmetry of every image is perfect. You feel as though you are right on deck for these moments. The variety of images in this volume is a special treat. It makes you wonder: How intently are crew members observing the surrounding images as they sail past? For all of us, we are lucky to see what Onne visualized through his camera.

Onne will depict a yacht in crisp detail and yet find a way to blur the water to enhance the feeling of movement. It would be easy to understand why Onne might keep his photographic methods secret, and yet he offers seminars to aspiring photographers. Great artists must feel very comfortable in their own abilities to be able to share their techniques with others. The tangible results of many of these methods are on display at a popular gallery—operated by Onne and his wife, Tenley—on the waterfront in Newport, Rhode Island. It is worth a visit. Few people leave empty-handed.

SAILING IS A SPORT THAT CAN BE PLAYED FOR AN ENTIRE LIFETIME.
NO OTHER SPORT SEEMS TO CONNECT THE GENERATIONS AS EASILY AS SAILING.

★ ★ ★ ★ ★

Onne, Tenley, and their three children, Read, Billy, and Adrian have cruised extensively on the waters off the coast of New England. While Newport is their home, Onne has traveled the world. He is a native of the Netherlands and grew up in South Africa. Legend has it that he learned to sail before he could walk. He set out for a life at sea in his early twenties and has since crossed the oceans many times. He has sailed as far north and as far south as a sailboat can carry you. Any time you spend time with Onne he always makes you feel comfortable. You can tell he is enjoying his work. His engaging manner has surely been helpful in his being welcomed aboard the world's most spectacular racing and cruising yachts.

Sailing is a sport that can be played for an entire lifetime. No other sport seems to connect the generations as easily as sailing. Fundamentally, sailing is all about the freedom to ply the inland, coastal, and offshore waters of our world. On the one hand, tradition is honored, and on the other hand, owners are always seeking innovations that create faster yachts. It is an interesting dynamic of blending the old and the new and of balancing between the artist and the scientist. Sailors tend to be extremely competitive people, and yet camaraderie and respect for each other are important attributes that sailors share. While looking at Onne's work keep these thoughts in mind. These attributes are evident in this volume. There are many words that come to mind when describing Onne's master work: unique, balanced, colorful, action-packed, symmetrical, beautiful, precise, detailed, fantasy-filled, businesslike, forward-moving, pleasant, purposeful, and fun. No doubt you can add your own list of words to describe the images in *Sailing America*.

The technical aspect of taking pictures has changed dramatically over the past forty years. Slides have given way to digital photography. The best cameras provide photographers with the tools to capture amazingly clear images. There is a considerable amount of science involved in photographic equipment these days. And yet the ability to place oneself in the perfect position to capture something unique rests with the artistic ability of the photographer. Onne van der Wal understands boats and people. He has raced at the highest levels of the sport, cruised on the most remote waters of the world, and photographed subjects from every possible vantage point. *Sailing America* rewards us with a cross section of American sailors, yachts, the sea, and the waterfront from one of the greatest photographers of our age.

GARY JOBSON

A

MAINE, MASSACHUSETTS, NEW HAMPSHIRE,
RHODE ISLAND & VERMONT

★ ★ ★ ★ ★

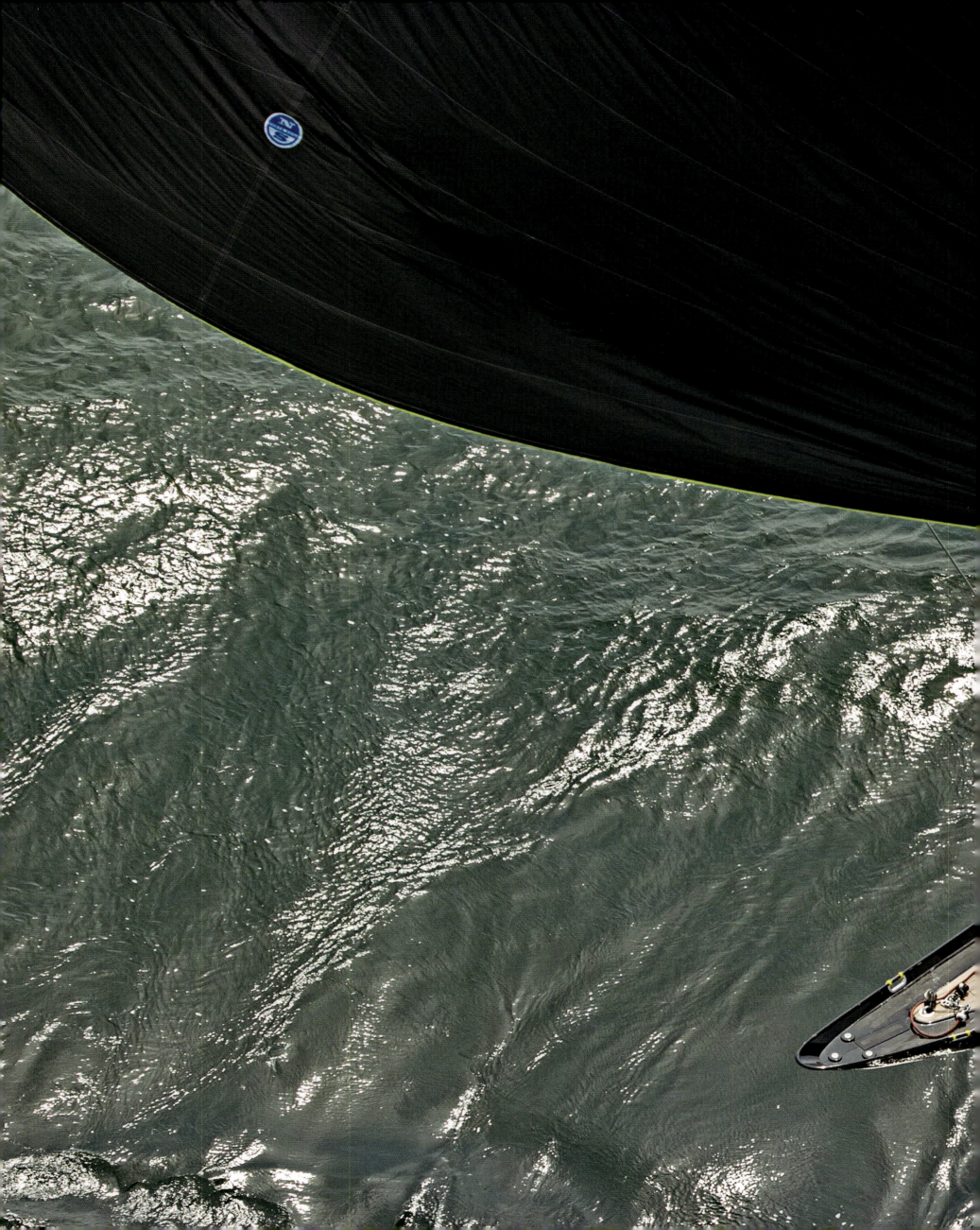

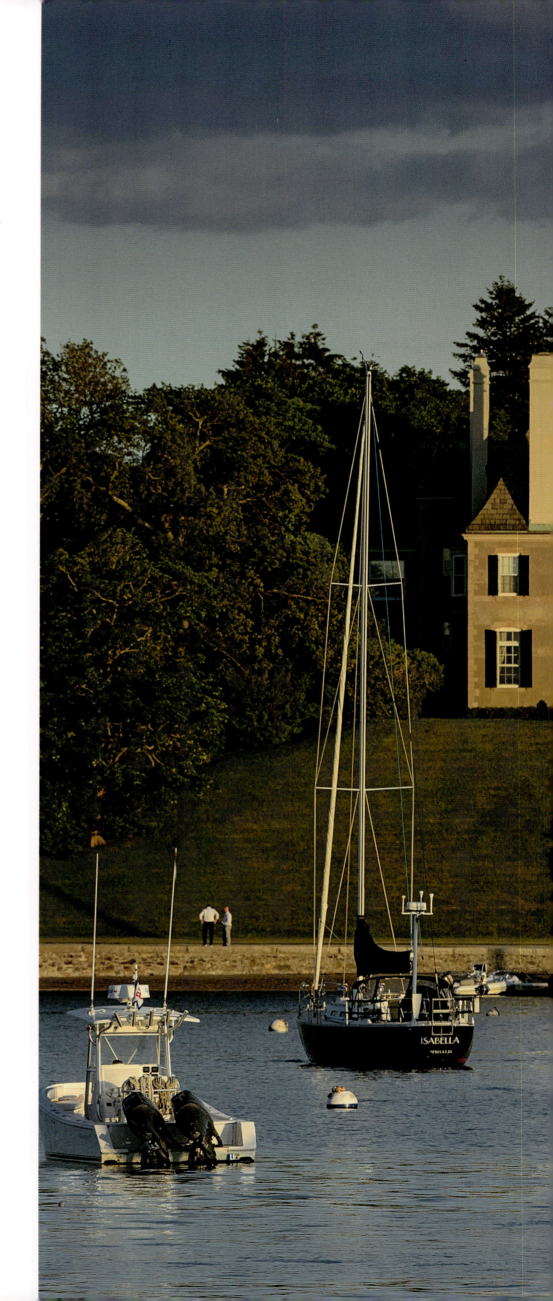

B

CONNECTICUT &
NEW YORK

★ ★ ★ ★ ★

C

DELAWARE, MARYLAND, NEW JERSEY, PENNSYLVANIA & VIRGINIA

★ ★ ★ ★ ★

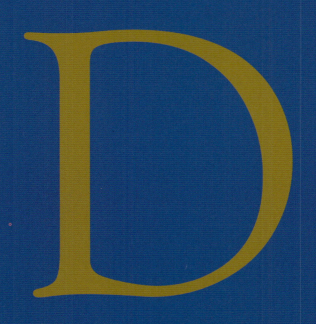

D

ALABAMA, ARKANSAS, FLORIDA, GEORGIA,
LOUISIANA, MISSISSIPPI, NORTH CAROLINA,
SOUTH CAROLINA & TENNESSEE

★ ★ ★ ★ ★

E

INDIANA, KENTUCKY, MICHIGAN,
OHIO & WEST VIRGINIA

★ ★ ★ ★ ★

F

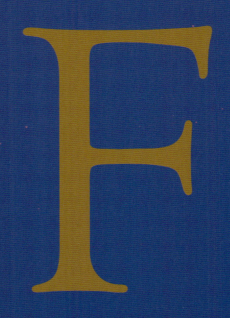

COLORADO, KANSAS, MISSOURI,
NEBRASKA, NEW MEXICO, OKLAHOMA,
TEXAS & WYOMING

★ ★ ★ ★ ★

G

NORTHERN CALIFORNIA
& NEVADA

★ ★ ★ ★ ★

H

HAWAII

★★★★★

J

ARIZONA,
SOUTHERN CALIFORNIA
& UTAH

★ ★ ★ ★ ★

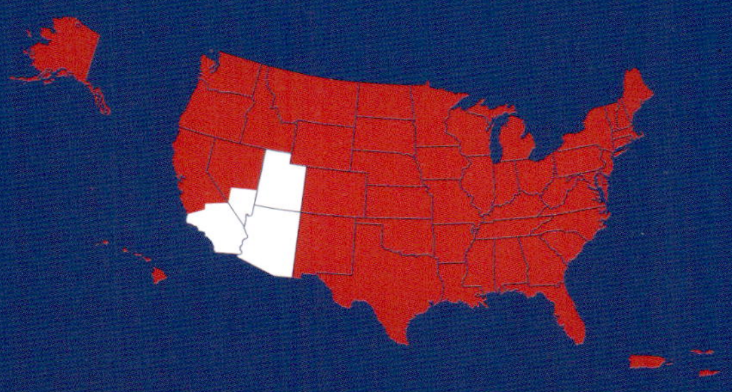

K

ILLINOIS, INDIANA, IOWA, MICHIGAN, MINNESOTA, MISSOURI, NORTH DAKOTA, SOUTH DAKOTA & WISCONSIN

★ ★ ★ ★ ★

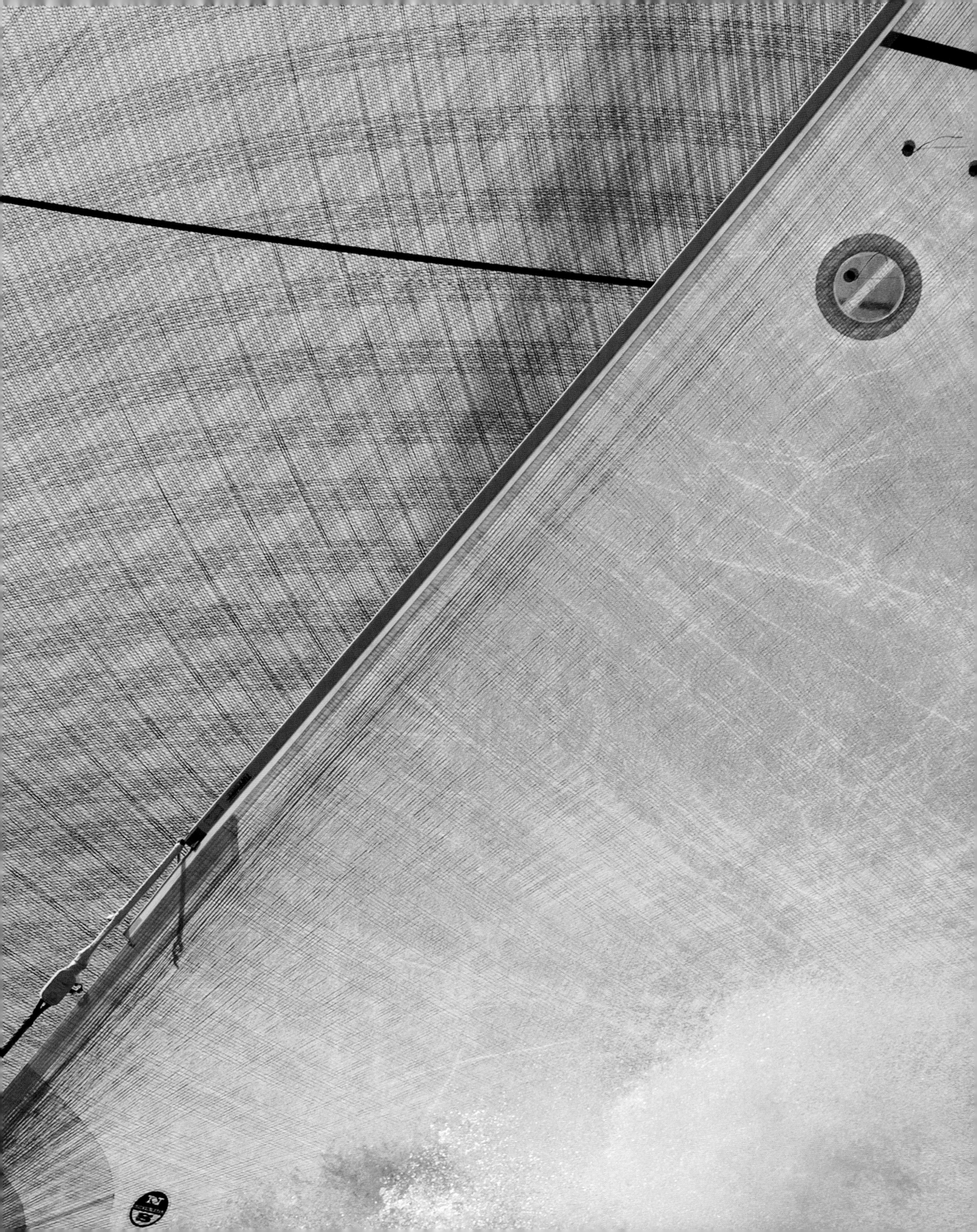

L

ALASKA, IDAHO, MONTANA,
OREGON & WASHINGTON

★ ★ ★ ★ ★

M

PUERTO RICO & U.S. VIRGIN ISLANDS

★ ★ ★ ★ ★

INDEX
OF IMAGES

PAGES 12-13
The foredeck crew prepares to douse
Hanuman's spinnaker at the leeward
mark during the 2017 J Class World
Championships in Newport, RI.
Canon EOS 5D Mark IV, 100-400mm lens,
f5.6, 1/1600, ISO 500

PAGE 14
A fleet of New York Yacht Club Sonars
reaching toward their leeward mark on
a beautiful fall evening.
Canon EOS R, 400mm lens,
f8, 1/1600, ISO 400

PAGE 15
Rose Island Lighthouse and the Newport
Bridge in the background behind a fleet
of Sonars racing during a New York Yacht
Club series.
Canon EOS R, 400mm lens,
f8, 1/800, ISO 400

PAGES 16-17
Ken Read at the helm of *Comanche*,
a 100-foot carbon fiber maxi yacht, at
the start of the Newport to Bermuda
Race in 2016.
Canon EOS 5D Mark III, 24-70mm lens,
f8, 1/3200, ISO 800

PAGE 24
Sheets and halyards on belaying pins
on the tall ship *Oliver Hazard Perry*.
Canon EOS 5D Mark III, 70-200mm lens,
f3.5, 1/2000, ISO 100

PAGE 25
Downwind sails of two classic yachts
during the Around the Island Race,
the oldest continual yacht race on
Narragansett Bay.
Canon EOS 5D Mark III, 100-400mm lens,
f8, 1/1600, ISO 400

PAGES 26-27
A beautifully lit Herreshoff S Boat
moored in front of the New York Yacht
Club's summer clubhouse, Harbor Court.
Canon EOS 1D X Mark II, 300mm lens,
f8, 1/2500, ISO 800

PAGE 28
The Oar restaurant, a popular spot
for crews to hang out after racing during
Block Island Race Week.
Canon EOS 1Ds Mark II, 15mm lens,
f4.5, 1/160, ISO 400

PAGE 34
A fleet of Swan 42s rounding the
top mark on Narragansett Bay during
the 2011 New York Yacht Club's
invitational Cup.
Canon EOS 1Ds Mark III, 70-200mm lens,
f5.6, 1/1250, ISO 200

PAGE 39
A J/111 punching its way to windward
off Beavertail, RI, in a blustery south-
westerly breeze.
Canon EOS 1Ds Mark III, 70-200mm lens,
f7.1, 1/1000, ISO 200

PAGES 40-41
The bow of KZ3 to leeward of KZ5
during the 2015 12-meter North American
Championships in Newport, RI.
Canon EOS 5D Mark III. 200mm lens,
f6.3, 1/2500, ISO 200

PAGE 42
Tilly, a 1912 German-built, gaff-rigged
sloop, racing in Newport's 2016 Classic
Yacht Regatta.
Canon EOS 5D Mark III, 24-70mm lens,
f9, 1/800, ISO 500

PAGES 48-49
A typical foggy sunrise over a fleet
of sailboats moored off the Hinckley
Company's dock in Southwest Harbor, ME.
Mamiya M7 Camera, Fuji RVP film

PAGE 50
A Morris M52 motoring home on a
still summer's night off Mount Desert
Island, ME.
Canon EOS 5D Mark II, 24-70mm lens,
f8, 1/60, ISO 200

PAGE 51
A Morris M36 sails into the sunset on
Somes Sound, ME.
Canon EOS -1Ds, 70-200mm lens,
f7.1, 1/640, ISO 100

PAGES 52-53
The lobster boat fleet at Bass Harbor, ME,
looking across toward Morris Yachts'
service yard.
Canon EOS 1DX, 24-70mm lens,
f6.3, 1/160, ISO 100

INDEX
OF IMAGES

PAGE 58
The *Mary D*, a Hinckley Bermuda 40, crosses tacks under another Hinckley during their 2003 Rendezvous in Somes Sound, ME.
Canon EOS 1Ds, 100-400mm lens, f10, 1/640, ISO 100

PAGE 59
Hinckley sailboats beating their way upwind during the 2003 Hinckley Rendezvous in Somes Sound, Maine.
Canon EOS 1Ds, 100-400mm lens, f8, 1/1000, ISO 100

PAGES 60-61
Surprise, a gaff-rigged Friendship sloop, sails past the Bear Island Light off Mount Desert Island, ME.
Canon EOS 1Ds, Mark II, 70-200mm lens, f7.1, 1/400, ISO 100

PAGES 62-63
Scheherazade, a Bruce King–designed 155-foot ketch, beating to weather on Frenchman Bay off Mount Desert Island, ME.
Canon EOS 1DX, 24-70mm lens, f11, 1/200, ISO 100

PAGES 70-71
Two Concordia yawls, part of a fleet of 103 designed in 1932 by Raymond Hunt, sailing downwind on Buzzards Bay, MA.
Canon EOS 1Ds, Mark III, 100-400mm lens, f9, 1/800, ISO 200

PAGES 72-73
A group of intrepid sailors breezes past Longpoint Light in their daysailer on a brisk fall afternoon in Provincetown, Cape Cod.
Canon EOS 1Ds Mark II, 300mm lens, f9, 1/320, ISO 100

PAGES 74-75
A Sonar maneuvers through the mooring field in Marblehead Harbor, MA, with the Corinthian Yacht Club in the background.
Canon EOS 1Ds, 24-70mm lens, f6.3, 1/400, ISO 100

PAGES 76-77
Boston Community Boating daysailers on a blustery fall afternoon on the Charles River, with downtown buildings as their backdrop.
Canon EOS 5D Mark IV, 100-400mm lens, f7.1, 1/640, ISO 200

PAGE 83
An aerial shot of three Concordias during the 70th Anniversary Regatta out of Padanaram, MA.
Canon EOS 1Ds Mark II, 100-400mm lens, f7.1, 1/800, ISO 200

PAGES 84-85
Classic wooden boats moored in Vineyard Haven on Martha's Vineyard, MA.
Canon EOS 1Ds, 24-70mm lens, f9, 1/500, ISO 100

PAGE 86
Snoek at anchor in Tarpaulin Cove, with a lone farmhouse on Naushon Island, the largest of the Elizabeth Islands, MA.
Canon EOS 5D Mark IV, 100-400mm lens, f5.6, 1/1600, ISO 400

PAGE 87
Snoek, a 1972 36-foot Pearson sloop, at anchor in Tarpaulin Cove on Naushon Island, MA.
Canon EOS 5D Mark IV, 70-200mm lens, f6.3, 1/1250, ISO 400

PAGES 98-99
Fall foliage serves as the backdrop for a lonely catboat on a mooring in Mill Cove, Wickford, RI.
Canon EOS 5D Mark III, 100-4000mm lens, f6.3, 1/640, ISO 200

PAGE 100
A Herrescoff 12.5 sails in Hadley's Harbor on the eastern end of Naushon Island, MA.
Canon EOS 1DX, 400mm lens, f6.3, 1/1600, ISO 640

PAGE 102
Three sunfish ghosting along after the start of the Wednesday evening races in Stonington, CT.
Canon EOS 5D Mark IV, 100-400mm lens, f7.1, 1/3200, ISO 400

PAGE 103
Island Girl reaches along under spinnaker to the finish line during the Wednesday night races in Stonington, CT.
Canon EOS 5D Mark IV, 100-400mm lens, f6.3, 1/1600, ISO 400

INDEX
OF IMAGES

PAGES 104-105
The Americas Cup World Series
held in New York City sailing on the
Hudson River.
*Canon EOS 5D Mark III, 24-70mm lens,
f7.1, 1/1600, ISO 400*

PAGE 106
A view of Ellis Island and the busy
New York Harbor with the skyline of
Manhattan in the background.
*Canon EOS 5D, 70-200mm lens,
f7.1, 1/500, ISO 100*

PAGE 107
Vivid, an 88-foot Jongert-built sloop,
sailing past the iconic Lady Liberty in
New York Harbor.
*Canon EOS 5D, 300mm lens,
f5.6, 1/800, ISO 100*

PAGE 108
Hugo Boss, an IMOCA racing-class yacht,
sailing under the Verrazzano-Narrows
Bridge in New York City.
*Canon EOS 1D X, 24-70mm lens,
f14, 1/400, ISO 400*

PAGES 114-115
Nathaniel Herreshoff designed the
12.5 in 1914 and a total of 364 were built at
Herreshoff through 1943. A fine example
is seen here sailing past Deering Point on
Shelter Island, NY.
*Canon EOS 5D Mark IV, 100-400mm lens,
f6.3, 1/1250, ISO 200*

PAGES 118-119
Two log canoes crossing tacks in the
Miles River off of St. Michael's, MD.
*Canon EOS 5D Mark IV, 70-200mm lens,
f6.3, 1/2500, ISO 400*

PAGE 120
A log canoe is a type of sailboat
developed in the Chesapeake Bay region.
Based on the dugout, it was the principal
traditional fishing boat of the bay, but now
is more famous as a racing sailboat.
*Canon EOS 5D Mark IV, 24-70mm lens,
f9, 1/30, ISO 400*

PAGE 121
A fleet of Tartan boats at the
annual United States Sailboat Show
in Annapolis, MD.
*Canon EOS-1DS, 24-70mm lens,
f8, 1/160, ISO 100*

PAGES 130-131
Brown pelicans fly past a pair of dueling
Lasers on Charleston Harbor, SC.
*Canon EOS 1Ds Mark III, 300mm lens,
f4.5, 1/1600, ISO 100*

PAGES 132-133
A fleet of Sunfish at a start during
the 2006 Sunfish World Championships
in Charleston, SC.
*Canon EOS 1Ds Mark II, 70-200mm lens,
f5.6, 1/1000, ISO 100*

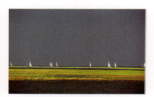

PAGES 134-135
A fleet of Tornados heads home from
racing during the 1996 Atlanta Olympic
Games, where the sailing was held off
Savannah, GA.
*Canon EOS 1v Camera, 70-200 mm lens,
Fuji Velvia film*

PAGES 136-137
An aerial view of *Numbers*, an IRC66,
racing upwind during the 2008 Miami
Grand Prix regatta.
*Canon EOS 1DS, Mark III Camera, Canon
300 mm f2.8L lens*

PAGE 144
The downwind fleet of Stars with Key
Biscayne in the background.
*Canon EOS 1Ds Mark III, 70-200mm lens,
f9, 1/640, ISO 200*

PAGE 145
A tight start to the Bacardi Cup
International Star Fleet, held annually
on Biscayne Bay in Miami, FL.
*Canon EOS 1Ds Mark III, 70-200mm lens,
f7.1, 1/1250, ISO 200*

PAGE 149
The Maxi 72, *Proteus*, dropping spinnaker
at the leeward mark during Key West Race
Week, FL.
*Canon EOS 5D Mark III, 70-200mm lens,
f7.1, 1/1250, ISO 200*

PAGE 150
A fleet of Stars, a 6.9-meter one-design
racing keel boat for two people designed
in 1910, hard on the wind with the skyline
of Miami in the background.
*Canon EOS 1Ds Mark III, 500mm lens,
f6.3, 1/2000, ISO 200*

PAGE 109
Alex Thompson sails *Hugo Boss* up the Narrows, a tidal strait between upper and lower New York Bay, in 2014.
Canon EOS 1D X, 24-70mm lens, f14, 1/640, ISO 400

PAGE 110
Francois Gabart, the skipper of *Macif*, sails under the Verrazzano-Narrows Bridge after finishing first on a solo transatlantic race from Plymouth, England, to New York City in 8 days, 8 hours, and 54 minutes—setting a new solo transatlantic record.
Canon EOS 5D Mark III, 24-70mm lens, f11, 1/15, ISO 200

PAGE 111
Macif, a 100-foot transatlantic trimaran, makes a victory loop around New York Harbor after the Transat Bakerly solo race in May, 2016.
Canon EOS 1D X Mark II, 70-200mm lens, f5, 1/80, ISO 5000

PAGES 112-113
A lone sailor weaves her way through a fleet of moored Herreshoff 12.5s at Shelter Island Yacht Club, New York.
Canon EOS 5D Mark IV, 100-400mm lens, f8, 1/250, ISO 200

PAGES 122-123
An intrepid fisherman heads out of Knapps Narrows for the day's catch, while a classic Skipjack sails along the horizon.
Canon EOS 1Ds, 70-200mm lens, f16, 1/500, ISO 100

PAGE 124
Mystery, barreling along with all her crew on the hiking board battling to keep her on an even keel.
Canon EOS 5D Mark IV, 70-200mm lens, f6.3, 1/2000, ISO 400

PAGE 125
The log canoe requires a large amount of human ballast to keep it upright.
A. Canon EOS 5D Mark IV, 70-200mm lens, f6.3, 1/2000, ISO 400 B)

PAGES 126-127
Persistence and *Island Blossom* race to the finish with their crews sitting out on the hiking boards acting as ballast.
Canon EOS 5D Mark IV, 70-200mm lens, f14, 1/640, ISO 400

PAGES 138-139
Bella Mente in a very good position minutes after a start during Key West Race Week, FL.
Canon EOS 5D, Mark III, 70-200mm lens, f6.3, 1/1250, ISO 200

PAGE 140
The one-design class of Swan 45s racing downwind in the milky water during Key West Race Week in 2006.
Canon EOS-1Ds Mark II, 400mm lens, f6.3, 1/1000, ISO 100

PAGE 141
Hap Fauth's Maxi 72, *Bella Mente*, reaching toward the leeward mark at Key West Race Week in 2016.
anon EOS 5D Mark III, 70-200mm lens, f7.1, 1/1250, ISO 200

PAGES 142-143
Sprits and sails of Optimist dinghies —the most popular type of junior sailing boat, with a worldwide fleet of more than 150,000.
Canon EOS 1Ds Mark II, 100-400mm lens, f7.1, 1/800, ISO 100

PAGE 151
A fleet of Stars rounding the windward mark during the annual Bacardi Cup, sailed on Biscayne Bay in Miami in 2012.
Canon EOS 1Ds Mark III, 300mm lens, f5.6, 1/800, ISO 100

PAGES 152-153
Spray washes off the bow of a 420 during the Great Oaks Invitational High-School Regatta at Southern Yacht Club in New Orleans, LA.
Canon EOS 5D Mark III, 100-400mm lens, f8, 1/6400, ISO 400

PAGES 154-155
420s parading past Southern Yacht Club after a hard day's sailing on Lake Ponchetrain during the 2015 Great Oaks Invitationals Regatta.
Canon EOS 5D Mark III, 200-560mm lens, f6.3, 1/800, ISO 250

PAGE 156
420s short tacking up the beat in a high traffic zone on Lake Pontchartrain during the Great Oaks Invitational Regatta in 2015.
Canon EOS 5D Mark III, 100-400mm lens, f8, 1/4000, ISO 400

INDEX
OF IMAGES

PAGE 157
The crew of this 420 get hosed by white water while working their way to windward on a blustery day on Lake Pontchartrain.
Canon EOS 5D Mark III, 200-560mm lens, f6.3, 1/5000, ISO 400

PAGES 158-159
A gaggle of Optis at the start on Lake Pontchartrain during the 2006 Optimist Midwinter Championships in New Orleans, LA.
Canon EOS 1Ds Mark II, 100-400mm lens, f7.1, 1/800, ISO 100

PAGES 162-163
The spray flies from the bow of the Huckins press boat while watching *Windquest* approaching the finish line of the 2018 Chicago Mackinac Race.
Canon EOS 5D Mark IV, 24-70mm lens, f7.1, 1/1600, ISO 4000

PAGES 164-165
Windquest powers along towards the finish under the Mackinac Bridge during the 2018 Mac Race, the oldest annual freshwater distance race in the world.
Canon EOS 5D Mark IV, 100-400mm lens, f6.3, 1/1600, ISO 4000

PAGES 174-175
Two VX skiffs crossing on the downwind leg on Lake Ray Hubbard in Dallas, TX.
Canon EOS 5D Mark III, 100-400mm lens, f10, 1/4000, ISO 400

PAGES 176-177
Moments after the start of a VX race at the Rush Creek Yacht Club on Lake Ray Hubbard, TX.
Canon EOS 1DX, 70-200mm lens, f7.1, 1/1250, ISO 200

PAGES 178-179
Two lone sailboats rest in Jenny Lake under the majestic watch of Grand Teton in Jackson, WY.
Canon EOS 5D Mark III, 70-200mm lens, f9, 1/1250, ISO 320

PAGES 182-183
Three Santana 22s ready to be launched from the pier of Stillwater Yacht Club, in the midst of the infamous Pebble Beach Golf Club.
Canon EOS 5D Mark IV, 16-35mm lens, f9, 1/400, ISO 200

PAGES 192-193
Bows of various small keel boats on their trailers at the Santa Cruz Yacht Club.
Canon EOS 5D Mark IV, 100-400mm lens, f6.3, 1/800, ISO 200

PAGE 194
A view of the crowded yard and docks from the deck of the Santa Cruz Yacht Club.
Canon EOS 5D Mark IV, 24-70mm lens, f9, 1/800, ISO 200

PAGE 195
Detail of teak rail and rope on a California registered sailboat, Santa Cruz Yacht Club.
Canon EOS 5D Mark IV, 100-400mm lens, f5, 1/1600, ISO 200

PAGES 196-197
A classic shields sailing past the iconic Monterrey Fish Company's dock in Monterrey harbor.
Canon EOS 5D Mark IV, 100-400mm lens, f7.1, 1/500, ISO 1600

PAGE 206
The Napali coast as viewed from the leeward rail onboard Sarasvati.
Canon EOS 5D Mark IV, 16-35mm lens, f9, 1/400, ISO 400

PAGE 207
The Napali coast as viewed from the leeward rail onboard Sarasvati.
Canon EOS 5D Mark IV, 16-35mm lens, f11, 1/125, ISO 400

PAGES 208-209
Sayonara and *Falcon 2000* racing in the 1994 Kenwood Cup off Oahu's famous volcanic icon, Diamond Head.
Canon EOS 1v Camera, 70-200mm lens, Fuji Velvia Film

PAGE 210
My wife, Tenley, admiring the splendor and scale of the beautiful Napali Coast while standing on the bow of Craig Hine's yacht, Sarasvati.
Canon EOS 5D Mark IV, 16-35mm lens, f11, 1/250, ISO 400

PAGE 166
Doug DeVos, skippering *Windquest*, an 86-foot Reichel Pugh–designed sloop, crosses the finish line of the 2018 Mac Race at Round Island Light.
Canon EOS 5D Mark IV, 100-400mm lens, f5.6, 1/320, ISO 6400

PAGE 167
Albatross, the first cruising boat to finish the 2018 Mac Race, approaching Round Island Light in the Straights of Mackinac, which connect Lake Michigan and Lake Huron.
Canon EOS 5D Mark IV, 100-4000mm lens, f5.6, 1/400, ISO 6400

PAGE 168-169
The silhouette of a bowman during a gybe on a sunset sail on Lake Erie.
Canon EOS 1v Camera, 14mm lens, Fuji RVP film

PAGES 172-173
A marina full of small lake boats at Rush Creek Yacht Club on Lake Ray Hubbard, TX.
Canon EOS 5D Mark III, 16-35mm lens, f9, 1/800, ISO 250

PAGES 184-185
The sun sets over a fleet of moored sailboats on Tomales Bay, just North of Marconi in Marin County, CA.
Canon EOS 5D Mark IV, 16-35mm lens, f7.1, 1/640, ISO 200

PAGES 186-187
A lone sailboat leaving San Francisco Bay heading past the Point Bonita Lighthouse.
Canon EOS 1Ds Mark III, 70-200mm lens, f8, 1/400, ISO 200

PAGES 188-189
Two small cruising boats sailing under the Golden Gate Bridge.
Canon EOS 1Ds Mark III, 300mm lens, f5.6, 1/1250, ISO 200

PAGES 190-191
Looking though the support cables of the Golden Gate Bridge from the Marin Headlands with the St. Frances Yacht Club and the skyline of San Francisco in the background.
Canon EOS 1Ds Mark III, 70-200mm lens, f7.1, 1/640, ISO 200

PAGES 198-199
The Shields fleet moments before their start of the evening beer can racing out of the Monterrey Peninsula Yacht Club.
Canon EOS 5D Mark IV, 16-35mm lens, f9, 1/1600, ISO 400

PAGE 200
Two Shields cross tacks during the Monterrey Peninsula Yacht Club's beer can racing series, April 2018.
Canon EOS 5D Mark IV, 100-400mm lens, f8, 1/1000, ISO 400

PAGE 201
The Monterrey Peninsula Yacht Club beer can racing fleet off Del Monte Beach, Monterey, CA.
Canon EOS 5D Mark IV, 100-400mm lens, f5, 1/2500, ISO 400

PAGES 204-205
A few sailboats at rest on a beautiful morning in Hanalei Bay, Kauai, HI.
Canon EOS 5D Mark IV, 16-35mm lens, f11, 1/250, ISO 400

PAGE 211
A fleet of colorful outriggers moored in the crystal clear water off the Outrigger Canoe Club, near Diamond Head in Honolulu.
Canon EOS 5D Mark IV, 24-70mm lens, f7.1, 1/400, ISO 400

PAGES 212-213
A rainbow appears along the Nepali coast after a heavy rain falls at Hanalei Bay, Kauai, Hawaii.
Canon EOS 5D Mark IV, 24-105mm lens, f7.1, 1/1250, ISO 400

PAGES 214-215
The colorful mountains of the Nepali coast in Kauai serve as the backdrop for *Serasvati's* afternoon sail.
Canon EOS 5D Mark IV, 24-105mm lens, f8, 1/160, ISO 400

PAGE 216
Looking up the leech of a Beneteau 46 during a sunset sail off the Napali Coast.
Canon EOS 5D Mark IV, 16-35mm lens, f11, 1/160, ISO 400

INDEX
OF IMAGES

PAGE 217
Sarasvati sails along the Napali coast while a threatening rain squall looms in the peaks behind her.
Canon EOS 5D Mark IV, 24-105mm lens, f8, 1/125, ISO 400

PAGES 220-221
A lone cruiser motor-sailing past White Cove on the East side of Santa Catalina Island, CA.
Canon EOS 5D Mark IV, 16-25mm lens, f9, 1/400, ISO 500

PAGES 222-223
Standing atop Mount Ada overlooking the mooring field in Avalon, Santa Catalina Island, CA.
Canon EOS 5D Mark IV, 24-70mm lens, f7.1, 1/2000, ISO 500

PAGES 224-225
California Dreaming, a team racing series held off Belmont Pier near Long Beach, CA.
Cabib EIS 5D Mark IV, 100-400mm lens, f8, 1/800, ISO 200

PAGES 230-231
A picturesque morning view of Moro Bay Rock, a volcanic plug at the entrance to Morro Bay Harbor. The rock is protected as part of the Moro Bay State Preserve.
Canon EOS 5D Mark IV, 100-400mm lens, f8, 1/6400, ISO 400

PAGES 232-233
Santa Barbara Youth Sailing Foundation practicing in their 420s off Santa Barbara Point.
Canon EOS 5D Mark IV, 100-400mm lens, f6.3, 1/4000, ISO 640

PAGE 234
A Catalina Capri 22 sailing through the Santa Barbara harbor with Stearns Wharf in the background.
Canon EOS 5D Mark IV, 100-400mm lens, f7.1, 1/2000, ISO 640

PAGE 235
Lazy harbor seals lying on the beach on Point Castillo in Santa Barbara, CA, watching the passing 420s.
Canon EOS 5D Mark IV, 100-400mm lens, f7.1, 1/2500, ISO 640

PAGE 245
Sailors rigging their A Class scow in preparation for the day's racing on Lake Minnetonka, MN.
Canon EOS 5D Mark IV, 70-200mm lens, f5, 1/1600, ISO 200

PAGES 246-247
Eagle and *Red Eye*, close reaching during the A Class Scow National Championships on Lake Minnetonka in June 2016.
Canon EOS 5D Mark IV, 70-200mm lens, f10, 1/6400, ISO 200

PAGES 248-249
The A Class Scow National Championships on Lake Minnetonka in June 2016.
Canon EOS 5D Mark IV, 70-200mm lens, f10, 1/6400, ISO 200

PAGES 252-253
Shaman, an 88-foot Bill Tripp–designed sloop, dwarfed by Bear Glacier in Kenai Fjords National Park.
A: Canon EOS 5d Mark IV, 100-400mm lens, f5, 1/4000, ISO 500 B: Canon EOS Canon EOS Iv Camera, 70-200mm lens, Fuji Velvia Film

PAGES 260-261
The main pier of the North Flathead Yacht Club on beautiful spring day.
Canon EOS 5D Mark IV, 24-70mm lens, f8, 1/800, ISO 200

PAGE 262
Rig details of *Nor'Easter*, the Herreshoff Q Boat built in 1928.
Canon EOS 5D Mark IV, 70-200mm lens, f2.8, 1/200, ISO 640 and Canon EOS 5D Mark IV, 70-200mm lens, f4.5, 1/80, ISO 1250

PAGE 263
Designed by L. Francis Herreshoff, Nathaniel's son, *Questa* was built to the standard set for racing the Americas Cup; here she is enjoying the mountain breeze in Montana.
Canon EOS 5D Mark IV, 100-400mm lens, f7.1, 1/3200, ISO 640

PAGE 267
Wooden boats alongside in Port Townsend, WA.
A) Canon EOS 5D Mark IV, 100-400mm lens, f7.1, 1/1000, ISO 500 B) Canon EOS 5D Mark IV, 100-400mm lens, f7.1, 1/400, ISO 500

PAGE 226
Minutes after the start at the Etchells Midwinters West in San Diego, CA, in April 2018.
Canon EOS 5D Mark IV, 100-400mm lens, f8, 1/2000, ISO 400

PAGE 227
Bruce Nelson's *Etchell's Rhino* during their Midwinters West Regatta in San Diego, CA.
Canon EOS 5D Mark IV, 100-400mm lens, f6.3, 1/4000, ISO 400

PAGE 228
Cruising boats moored in Moro Bay captured from Bayshore Bluffs Park.
Canon EOS 5D Mark IV, 100-400mm lens, f8, 1/800, ISO 200

PAGE 229
A few tenders on the beach at Bay Shore Bluffs, with the spectacular Moro Rock in the background.
Canon EOS 5D Mark IV, 16-35mm lens, f11, 1/400, ISO 200

PAGES 238-239
The start of the Beneteau 36.7 Class in the 2017 Chicago Mackinac Race, a 333-mile annual yacht race starting in Lake Michigan, IL, and ending in Lake Huron, off Mackinac Island, MI.
Canon EOS 5D Mark IV, 70-200mm lens, f6.3, 1/1250, ISO 200

PAGE 241
Wizard, a 74-foot Reichel Pugh–designed sloop, at the start of the 2017 Chicago Mackinac Race, which was first run in 1898 and is the oldest annual freshwater distance race in the world.
Canon EOS 5D Mark IV, 100-400mm lens, f6.3, 1/2000, ISO 400

PAGES 242-243
420s lined up on the dock at Lake Minnetonka Yacht Club.
Canon EOS 5D Mark IV, 70-200mm lens, f5, 1/2500, ISO 200

PAGE 244
The A Class scow, *Valkyrie*, ghosting along toward the starting line on Lake Minnetonka, MN.
Canon EOS 5D Mark IV, 70-200mm lens, f5, 1/1250, ISO 200

PAGES 254-255
Klepper kayaks stacked on the deck of *Shaman*, as she motors toward the setting sun in Alaska.
Canon EOS 1v Camera, 16-35mm lens, Fuji Velvia Film

PAGE 256
An A Class scow punches its way to windward on a blustery day on Lake Minnetonka.
Canon EOS 5D Mark IV, 100-400 lens, f6.3, 1/2500, ISO 640

PAGE 257
Questa, an L. Francis Herreshoff–designed Q Class Yacht built in 1929, sailing on Flathead Lake, MT.
Canon EOS 5D Mark IV, 100-400mm lens, f7.1, 1/1250, ISO 640

PAGE 258-259
Flathead Lake Lodge is the proud owner of two Herreshoff–designed Q Boats, but only Questa was out on the water on a beautiful June evening.
Canon EOS 5D Mark IV, 100-400mm lens, f7.1, 1/2000, ISO 640

PAGES 268-269
A cruiser on Admiralty Inlet, Port Townsend, WA, sailing towards a snow-capped Mount Baker.
Canon EOS 5D Mark IV, 100-400mm lens, f9, 1/1000, ISO 500

PAGES 270-271
The graceful lines of *Questa*'s stem, a 51-foot Q class racing sloop, plowing through the water in Flathead Lake, MT.
Canon EOS 5D Mark IV, f5, 1/1000, ISO 400

PAGES 272-273
A single windsurfer sails to leeward of the Melges 24 NorAm Championships on the Columbia River, OR.
Canon EOS 5D Mark IV, 200mm lens, f6.3, 1/2000, ISO 400

PAGE 274
Melges 24s sailing on the Columbia River, which divides Washington and Oregon.
Canon EOS 5D Mark IV, 70-200mm lens, f5.6, 1/3200, ISO 400

INDEX
OF IMAGES

PAGE 275
A fleet of Melges 24s on their upwind leg while racing on the Columbia River near Hood River, OR.
Canon EOS 5D Mark IV, 200mm lens, f6.3, 1/1600, ISO 400

PAGES 276-277
The rustic Port Townsend's waterfront, behind a cruiser at anchor.
Canon EOS 5D Mark IV, 100-400mm lens, f9, 1/1000, ISO 500

PAGE 278
Details of rope work on wooden boats in Port Townsend, WA.
A) Canon EOS 5d Mark IV, 100-400mm lens, f5, 1/4000, ISO 500 B) Canon EOS 5D Mark IV, 100-400mm lens, f7.1, 1/3200, ISO 500

PAGE 279
A beautiful wooden dory on the beach near Port Townsend, WA, with Mount Rainier in the background.
Canon EOS 5D Mark IV, 100-400mm lens, f7.1, 1/1250, ISO 500

PAGES 288-289
An over/under shot of the bow of *Wanderbird* while swimming in the lovely water off of Culebra, PR.
Canon EOS 5D Mark II, 15mm, f/18, 1/180, ISO 400

PAGE 290
A little Sunfish sails past a small heart shaped island off Fajardo, PR.
Canon EOS 1v, Fuji Velvia Film

PAGE 291
An aerial view of a lone catamaran anchored at Cayo Diablo in the Arrecifes de la Cordillera Natural Reserve, PR.
Canon EOS 1v, Fuji Velvia Film

PAGE 292
Young Adrian keeps watch from the bow of a charter catamaran as we are passed by a motoring sloop in the US Virgin Islands.
Canon EOS 5D, 16-35mm lens, f9, 1/100, ISO 100

GATEFOLD 1
During the Classic Yacht Regatta in 2013, the 12-meter *Valient* and a classic 6-meter cross tacks in front of Castle Hill Light.
Canon EOS 1DX, EF 200-400mm lens, f/6.3, 1/2500, ISO 500

GATEFOLD 2
The Etchells fleet on the downwind leg during their 2013 North American
Canon EOS 1DX, 400mm lens, f6.3, 1/2500, ISO 250

GATEFOLD 3
Two sloops sailing in front of Port Townsend, WA, with the majestic Cascade Mountains in the background.
Canon EOS 5D Mark IV, 100-400mm lens, f8, 1/1600, ISO 500

COVER
The elegant M29 daysailer, the smallest of M Series daysailers built by Morris, reaching along just before sunset on Biscayne Bay, Miami.
Canon EOS 1Ds Mark III, 70-200mm lens, f3.5, 1/320, ISO 100

BACK COVER
Intrepid during the 2015 12-Meter North Americans held in Newport with *American Eagle* and *Nefertiti* in the distance.
Canon EOS 5D Mark III, 24-70 mm lens, f9, 1/800, ISO 200

PAGES 282-283
A beautiful bay on the North side
of Culebrita, a small island East
of Culebra, PR (also known as the
Spanish Virgin Islands).
*Canon EOS 1Ds Mark III,16-35mm lens
f14, 1/1600 ISO 200*

PAGES 284-285
Looking over the bow of *Wanderbird* at
the North side of Culebrita, PR.
*Canon EOS 1Ds Mark III, 16-35mm lens,
f9, 1/200, ISO 200*

PAGE 286
Sunrise on *Wanderbird* while cruising
near Culebra, PR.
*Canon EOS 1Ds Mark III, 14mm lens,
f9, 1/60, ISO 200*

PAGE 287
A headstay detail with jib hanks
on *Wanderbird*, a beautifully converted
90-foot North Sea trawler.
*Canon EOS 1Ds Mark III, 14mm lens,
f7.1, 1/80, ISO 200*

PAGE 293
Read and Billy simultaneously
dive off the bows of a 46-foot charter
catamaran in the US Virgin Islands.
*Canon EOS 1Ds Mark II, 70-200mm lens,
f11, 1/200, ISO 100*

PAGES 294-295
A rainbow sets on the US Virgin
Islands while a lone Moorings charter
boat sits quietly at anchor.
*Canon EOS 1D, 70-200mm lens,
f5, 1/800, ISO 100*

First published in the United States of America in 2019 by
Rizzoli International Publications, Inc.
300 Park Avenue South
New York, NY 10010
www.rizzoliusa.com

Copyright © 2019 Onne van der Wal
Introduction: Gary Jobson

Publisher: Charles Miers
Editor: Jacob Lehman
Design by Opto
Design Coordinator: Olivia Russin
Production Manager: Colin Hough-Trapp
Managing Editor: Lynn Scrabis

All rights reserved. No part of this publication may be reproduced,
stored in a retrieval system, or transmitted in any form or by
any means, electronic, mechanical, photocopying, recording, or
otherwise, without prior consent of the publishers.

Printed in Hong Kong

2024 2025 2026 2027 / 10 9 8 7 6 5 4 3

ISBN: 978-0-8478-6358-7
Library of Congress Control Number: 2019943669

Visit us online:
Facebook.com/RizzoliNewYork
Twitter: @Rizzoli_Books
Instagram.com/RizzoliBooks
Pinterest.com/RizzoliBooks
Youtube.com/user/RizzoliNY
Issuu.com/Rizzoli